# RobertaFlack

text            **Charles and Ann Morse**
illustrations   **Dick Brude**
design concept  **Mark Landkamer**

published by    **Creative Education**
                **Mankato, Minnesota**

Published by Creative Educational Society, Inc.,
123 South Broad Street, Mankato, Minnesota 56001
Copyright © 1975 by Creative Educational Society, Inc. International
copyrights reserved in all countries.
No part of this book may be reproduced in any form without written permission
from the publisher. Printed in the United States.
Distributed by Childrens Press, 1224 West Van Buren Street, Chicago, Illinois 60607

Library of Congress Number: 74-13938     ISBN: 0-87191-396-8
Library of Congress Cataloging in Publication Data
Morse, Charles.     Roberta Flack.
1. Flack, Roberta—Juvenile literature. I. Morse, Ann, joint author.
II. Keely, John, illus.   III. Title.
ML3930.F54M7     784'.092'4 [B] 74-13938
ISBN 0-87191-396-8

"Ain't No Mountain High Enough," sang Roberta. The crowd caught hold of Roberta's song — people who were scrambling for parking places a few minutes before, people who had been waiting for hours just to see and hear Roberta. All these people were catching the spirit of Roberta Flack. They heard the message behind all Roberta's songs — things are possible with a little love, with a little kindness.

Washington, D.C., had declared Saturday, April 22, 1972, Roberta Flack/Human Kindness Day. The city of power was honoring the musical power of one of their own. Big things and simple things were planned for the day.

The big events included a parade to the Washington Monument, a champagne social given by the Black Caucus, awards and speeches, and a presentation ceremony in which the mayor would give Roberta the key to the city.

The simple plans were perhaps more powerful. School children were writing essays on human kindness. At a neighborhood center young artists would show their paintings of life as it might be. Young musicians would be singing their songs to Roberta's people.

Then it rained. It rained on Roberta's parade, cancelling it. It rained on speeches, cancelling many of them. It rained on the gold brocade, making the outside decorations droop. Only Roberta's song and the simple things could not be washed away.

It rained early at the Kennedy Center where a Roberta Flack breakfast was held. At 8 o'clock, sleepy people from the press and leaders of local arts organizations gathered. They waited for an hour for the guest of honor and wished they could get at the hot coffee they kept sniffing.

# Human Kindness Day

7

Finally, the hostess mumbled something about having the few words after breakfast and brought the guests to their eggs and sausage. Coffee was being passed around the second time when Roberta and a flock of her relatives and friends arrived. It was 9:30.

The hostess began her introduction. "I want to thank you all for getting up so early this morning . . ."

"All of us can't," Roberta interrupted in a loud, clear voice. The guests began to laugh and soon forgot they were eating cold toast and cold eggs. People began to exchange stories about Roberta. In a short time it seemed that a crowd of a hundred people became a group of Roberta's friends. The rain couldn't cancel the humor and spirit of the day.

Despite the rain, tribute was paid to Roberta. The young artists' show went on at the neighborhood's Gallery 1. A congressman's wife gave a cocktail party in Roberta's honor. A luncheon was held at Mr. Henry's, the local club where Roberta started her career as a performer.

The next day, in front of the Lincoln Memorial in Sylvan Park, a stage was set. Local children made a backdrop of painted hearts and faces and letters. The Mayor of Washington offered Roberta the key to the city. "She's made it, but she's never forgotten us," he said.

City officials and an arts promotion group called "Compared To What " had planned Roberta Flack Day. The mostly black audience, numbering in the thousands, waited impatiently for their star. Impatiently they waited through the mayor's speech and through the music of many unkowns. Then Roberta appeared and gave the awards to the children for their essays on human kindness. The crowd grew quiet.

One woman on stage. One woman in command of the day. One woman symbolizing the way to make it to the top — through training and discipline; by working with and caring for, not stepping on, the people along the way.

"Go up, Moses, you been down too long," Roberta began. Roberta tells her people to "Let Pharaoh go." The audience simmers; Roberta's quiet fire catches and spreads.

Roberta Flack/Human Kindness Day
April 22, 1972
Washington, D.C.

# In Person

Head back, eyes closed, a look of concentration and power on her face, Roberta Flack cries out for "Sister Jones — who didn't live another day;" not a cry of frenzy, but of understanding, a cry that's born into a song. The people, sitting attentively at Mr. Henry's Club in Washington, generously applaud Roberta's performance. Roberta's pleased smile shows the graciousness of a person who has performed well for people she cares about. A critic has said that she tries to let nothing come between the listener and the experience of the song.

"I'm a very giving performer; I really give, and it comes back to me."

Every song Roberta chooses to sing has to have meaning for her. The song has to do one thing: it has to move her. Roberta's approach to every song is very personal. When people have asked her how she can sing about things she hasn't experienced, Roberta says simply, "I become whatever it is I'm singing. It's not what you

10

say, it's the way you put pain on that thing that makes the difference."

Roberta goes from song to song, from challenge to challenge, and gives each experience all her effort.

After making her first recordings, Roberta dived into the new world of producing recordings. And to Roberta, the job meant more than just being a producer. It often meant being the musician, arranger, lyricist and sometimes the chief-in-charge of encouragement for the group making the record. Now Roberta runs Roberta Flack Enterprises which include a publishing company, a talent agency and a production company.

At home in a very fashionable part of Arlington, Virginia, Roberta is queen of an animal kingdom. There are often at least 10 cats — Persian, Siamese, alley cats and various other kinds. There are 3 or 4 dogs lumbering about the large, rambling house.

For over 7 years Roberta was married to Steve Novosel, a white jazz bassist. Except for a pop festival one summer, Roberta and Steve almost never played music together. The hard life on the concert tours, the separations that come with success, the racial pressure were struggles they both worked hard to overcome. In the early 1970's, Roberta told a magazine reporter, "It was rough at first. His family disowned him. My brother refused to give me away." They weathered many storms in those years. But in 1972 Roberta and Steve were divorced.

Now Roberta's mother lives with her. Mrs. Flack loves to cook and take care of the many needs of Roberta's pets. She'll play hymns on the piano to relax her daughter. Mrs. Flack is a pillar of strength to Roberta.

"I'm just like the songs I sing — loving, gullible,

supersensitive, extremely emotional,'' Roberta says. ''That's what it's all about, love — in all kinds of shapes and sizes and forms.'' Whether with an interviewer or a friend, Roberta is always herself.

A DJ once asked, ''What does music mean to you? Is it a profession, is it a creative urge, is it a life-style or what is it?''

Roberta answered, ''It's a life-style that's very, very definite. It's all those things . . . It's life and breath and it's love and beauty and all those delicious things. It is everything.

''I think it's only when an artist realizes *that,* then he can begin to know his potential for achievement, success and greatness.''

Roberta has never taken a drug to reach her high in music. She has very little time for musicians who resort to drugs. Still, Roberta knows that she has hang-ups, too. She feels that she eats too much and smokes too much. But she feels there is a difference between those habits and a drug habit. She doesn't *have* to eat or smoke before she sings.

''You need to be in good health,'' Roberta says. Sometimes when she comes home from a tour and she feels worn out, she says, ''I know I've eaten too many glazed doughnuts and not enough broccoli.''

''You have to be dedicated to whatever you consider your art.'' Roberta is constantly pulled between people's requests for old songs and her desire to try some newer ones. Roberta seeks a balance somewhere in between.

It's inside herself that Roberta finds resources. When she sings, her eyes are closed. It seems that then she can see the emotion of the song better.

''All you have to do is really to be honest with yourself,

to see whatever that thing is inside of you that keeps you turning. I think that to go there and to really become involved with yourself is the best thing that a musician or a person can possibly do."

Roberta is intent on being truthful. "People today are ready to hear the truth. If they like me, it's because of what I represent — my true self. All I want is to become a bigger and a better person — from head to toe."

# On Record

Les McCann, the jazz-pianist, described his experience of hearing Roberta Flack for the first time.

"It was a good thing that I'd found a seat before she took her place at the piano and sang her first note, because my knees would never have made it standing. Her voice touched, tapped, trapped and kicked over every emotion I've ever known. I laughed, cried and screamed for more."

Roberta remembers another night — a very rainy night — when Les McCann came to hear her. He came with a tape recorder under his coat and asked Roberta if he could record her. He did, and then he carried that tape all over the country. Roberta became known even before she started recording. "He was the one who made the right contacts and told me that Atlantic Records was interested in me. He's beautiful," Roberta told a magazine reporter.

McCann knew that Joel Dorn of Atlantic Records would recognize Roberta's talent as he had. Dorn had many people tell him about Roberta Flack. "Another Aretha. Another Nina Simone," they would say. Since Dorn already had Aretha Franklin on Atlantic Records,

he wasn't interested in anyone who sounded like her.

But when Less McCann played Roberta's tape for Joel Dorn, Atlantic's producer listened. He really listened. He heard, not an Aretha, not a Nina, but a different person. He heard the pure tones of Roberta Flack.

Roberta learned a great deal while making that first record, *"First Take."* She thought she knew all the necessary things. Roberta had always been excellent at selecting material. She had all the rhythmics down. And Roberta had an idea of what she wanted to hear as background to her voice. She thought that was enough.

But it wasn't. Roberta needed another ear, Joel Dorn's ear. Through Dorn, Roberta learned that there is a definite distinction between the musician and the producer. She felt that she could have ruined her recordings because "I would have had 12,000 strings and Leonard Bernstein conducting."

Joel Dorn feels good about Roberta's *"First Take."* Even though on that album there were technical mistakes which took him months to fix, he finds a kind of magic in it — a magic that would be hard to capture again. "For each LP," Dorn says, "you have to create a different psychological atmosphere."

The "First Take" album came out in 1969. It took a few years before it began to sell well. It wasn't until 1972 that Roberta received a gold record for "The First Time Ever I Saw Your Face." In 1971 Actor Clint Eastwood used the song in his DJ movie, *"Play Misty for Me."* Eventually, DJs who had seen the movie began playing the record on their shows.

It's now a fact that "The First Time Ever I saw Your Face" is one of Roberta's finest pieces. Composed by Ewan MacColl, it was first done at a fast tempo by two groups. But when Roberta sang it, a reporter for the *"Rolling Stone"* newspaper said, "Roberta blows the song at the listener in her aching snail's pace; and when it builds, it becomes a cloud under you, lifting you, and with room for two."

Roberta knows where to find fuel to keep her quiet fire glowing. Eugene McDaniels has given Roberta some of her best songs—"Compared To What," "Sunday and Sister Jones," a moving story of love and death, and "Reverend Lee" which some critics call a minor classic.

When Roberta does something satirical and mocking like "Reverend Lee," she plays with the song and tosses it out for the audience to play with it, too. In her second album, *"Chapter Two,"* Roberta introduces Reverend Lee as a "very big, strong, black, sexy Southern Baptist minister" who falls under the influence of Satan's daughter. Swinging through verses, Roberta sings out the fact that even "right" people can fall.

Donny Hathaway, a performer himself, sent Roberta one of his songs, "Our Ages Or Our Hearts" just after she signed with Atlantic Records. Roberta also did Hathaway's "Gone Away" on the *"Chapter Two"* album.

Having worked together on songs for Roberta's

18

albums, Hathaway and Roberta decided to do an album together in 1972. Their rendition of "You've Got A Friend" provided strong competition for James Taylor's hit.

The "Roberta Flack & Donny Hathaway" album illustrates the range of Roberta's talent. She wrote the song, "Be Real Black For Me," along with Hathaway and Charles Mann. She also wrote a long instrumental piece entitled "Mood." On that album there are likewise a number of Roberta's arrangements. She does the singing and plays either piano or organ accompaniment.

Roberta spends a great deal of time on each album. "Quiet Fire" took 15 months on and off. Joel Dorn doesn't mind taking years to do a song right. He says he has enough material on tape to put out a Roberta Flack album every 6 months, but he won't. Dorn has said, "Everything is going to come slowly, and everything is going to be right."

In "Killing Me Softly With His Song," Roberta's 1973 album, she won another gold record for the title song. "Jesse," is another big hit on the album. In that song, Roberta makes the listener feel with her the pain of loneliness that Jesse creates.

Roberta once told a reporter, "I can feel a song with

19

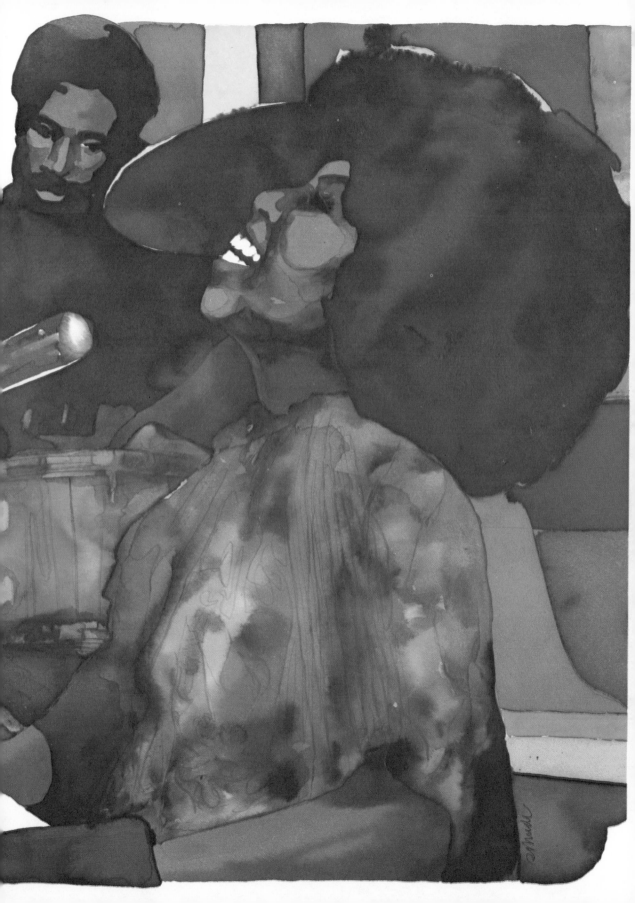

my hands and see it with my eyes, really see the scene." In her recordings, Roberta tries to make the listeners see the song with their eyes and almost feel the song in their hands.

# Flashback

Roberta Flack did not become a star overnight. She began to prepare for stardom ever since she was 4 years old.

Roberta was born in Black Mountain, North Carolina, in 1940. She has said that two preachers came from Black Mountain — Billy Graham and herself. "He's preaching in his way, and I'm preaching in my way."

When Roberta was 5, her family moved to Arlington, Virginia, just across the river from Washington, D.C. The Flacks lived in Green Valley, the black section of Arlington.

When she was 4 years old, Roberta played piano by ear. Her mother, Irene, worked as a cook for the public schools and played the organ at the local church. Roberta's father, Laron Flack, worked as a draftsman for the Veteran's Administration. Both parents loved the piano and encouraged Roberta's playing even during her youngest years.

Roberta remembers sitting on her mother's lap at the piano and fingering the keys. Mr. Flack had taught himself how to play the piano. Though he never played professionally, Roberta says that his music "came from his heart."

The Flack family's first year in Arlington was long and quiet. They didn't have a piano. But in time, Mr. Flack managed to find an old piano in the junk yard. It smelled bad. It was dirty. But Roberta's father cleaned it up,

painted it lime green, and it became the piano that Roberta learned to play on.

Roberta was 9 when Mrs. Alma Blackmon introduced her to her first piano lesson. Mrs. Blackmon was a friend of Mrs. Flack and an excellent piano teacher.

She taught Roberta for 4 years. When Roberta started with Mrs. Blackmon, she was already playing well. It wasn't long, therefore, before Mrs. Blackmon gave Roberta very difficult pieces to play — Beethoven sonatas and Rachmaninoff preludes.

Hazel Harrison, the first prominent woman Negro pianist, introduced the 12-year-old Roberta to Bach and Scarlatti. At 13, Roberta won second place in a segregated scholarship contest by playing a Scarlatti sonata.

The Flacks wanted their children to have a good education, so they sent them into Washington for grade school. Roberta remembers that she and her brother would each receive a nickel to ride the bus home.

But instead of the bus ride, the two young Flacks would often pool their nickels and buy a large, juicy sour dill pickle and a long peppermint candy stick. Roberta would poke out the center of the peppermint stick. Then she and her brother would use it as a straw to suck the juice out of the pickle. "Sweet and sour — right there," Roberta laughed. It was often after dark when the two got home.

Roberta was considered a good student in junior and senior high school. Besides music, Roberta liked algebra and psychology and anything that had to do with the occult. She says that she has had some psychic experiences. When she was young, Roberta enjoyed hearing the many strange stories her grandmother would tell. She says that the family rarely went to the doctor; their grandmother had herbs to cure every ache and pain.

There was little social life for Roberta in high school. "I was a good student because I didn't do anything else." Roberta weighed over 200 pounds then. She said all she did was play the piano, eat, study and go to church.

Roberta always had little singing groups going. She would often arrange music and direct her brother and 2 sisters. She would frequently organize rhythm and blues groups in the church basement.

At 15 Roberta graduated from high school and won a scholarship to Howard University in Washington. At 16, she assisted the Dean of Music with the choir. After graduating from Howard at 19, Roberta directed her first major piece — the opera Aida, in Washington.

Roberta's sensitivity about her weight caused her to change her course of study in college. When Roberta entered Howard, she concentrated mainly on the piano. Then she decided to study music education. This meant that she had to learn musical instruments, a study which led to an eye-opening experience.

In her third year at Howard, Roberta saw a picture of the school band with herself in the front row. Later Roberta talked about this incident with a magazine interviewer. "Honey, my cheeks were all puffed out, and you couldn't tell where I ended and the baritone horn started."

That's when Roberta began her course to lose weight. She dropped music education so she wouldn't have to use those bulky instruments, and then changed to vocal supervision.

In 1959, Roberta went on to graduate school. But when her father died that year, Roberta quit to get a job and help out with the family finances.

The young musician went to teach in Farmville, North

Carolina, a rural community in the eastern part of the state. It was the only black school in the area with 2,800 students ranging from pre-school through 12th grade. There was no money for a music teacher, so Roberta, who was hired to teach English literature, ended up teaching both subjects.

It was a poor school, depressing in many ways. But Roberta loved the kids. She taught them all. With her pitch pipe and auto harp, she went from room to room — teaching the youngest to the oldest.

Though the school was poor, many of the kids not only finished but went on to college. Some of them even earned masters' degrees. Roberta likes to think she had something to do with that.

As much as she liked the Farmville community, Roberta commuted to Washington every weekend. After a year in the rural school, she felt she had enough and returned to D.C. to get her Washington teaching certificate.

Roberta spent almost 8 years teaching music in various junior high schools in Washington. She liked teaching, loved the kids, but hated the paper work. Always she kept her fingers in performing or directing.

She played organ, conducted choirs, and coached voice students of Frederick Wilkerson. Later, Roberta took lessons from Wilkerson. He was to have a major part to play in her new career.

By 1962, Roberta had begun to moonlight. Besides holding down her teaching job, she took the chance to accompany a group of opera singers at the Tivoli Opera Restaurant in Georgetown, an exclusive section of Washington.

It was a heavy schedule for Roberta. She would teach

all day, run home for a quick nap and then play at Tivoli's until 2 a.m.

When business was good at Tivoli's, Roberta's friend Alma Blackmon played in the main room; Roberta played in the back room. When business slowed down a bit, Roberta would play the requests of the waiters. They'd ask for rhythm and blues pieces and for popular songs. And Roberta gave them everything they wanted.

The owner of Tivoli's heard some of Roberta's popular "stuff," and suggested she play it some night. One Christmas Roberta got her nerve up.

She began with "Chestnuts roasting on an open fire
. . ." Though the song was a long way from opera, the
crowd loved it. The Tivoli customers were in a holiday
mood and begged Roberta for more. She went on with
more songs. She did imitations of Carmen McRae and
Judy Garland. Then she went back to herself. She enjoyed
seeing the people enjoy her.

Voice teacher Frederick Wilkerson had been coach-
ing Roberta all during this time. After 3 years, he gave
her his decision: a classical artist? No. A good pop
performer? Yes. Roberta was shocked and hurt and didn't

go back to his studio for a month. She had always wanted to be a concert pianist and vocalist.

Yet it wasn't long before Roberta's fascination with pop music turned her career around. She accepted Wilkerson's advice. At the end of the 1967 school year, Roberta quit teaching.

Henry Yaffe, the new owner of Tivoli's, now called Mr. Henry's in Georgetown, was very much impressed with Roberta's popular style. That summer he invited her to play at his other restaurant in Washington, Mr. Henry's on Capitol Hill. Roberta sang and played 4 hours on Sunday afternoons for $20.

At that time the hardest thing for Roberta was getting used to a loud and impolite audience. Once in a while, Roberta would call out, "Can we have a little quiet at Table Five, please?" Frederick Wilkerson would encourage her. "Someday they'll listen," he said.

Eventually they did. Roberta's name spread by word of mouth. Mr. Yaffe, astounded at the lines of people coming to hear Roberta, built a room upstairs as a showcase for his discovery. Fittingly, he called the room, "Roberta's." Many famous performers like Pearl Bailey and Duke Ellington had to leave Washington to make it big, but Roberta was beginning to carve out her niche there.

On the *"Chapter Two"* album, musician Jerry Butler described the scene at Mr. Henry's. "She walked out unannounced and sat at her piano; and a small, noisy bar full of what seemed to be Sunday afternoon idlers, drinking beer and eating sandwiches, became a very quiet, attentive congregation.

"It was my first time in this place," the musician continues. "But I knew we were about to share something beautiful, and I felt at home.

"She touched the piano, and you knew from the response that years of practice and love had preceded that touch.

"Roberta sang, and she made our hearts sing.

"And when she was through, we all thanked her . . . And she in return thanked us with a smile so warm and natural that it seemed to be directed at me alone.

"In a moment we had become friends for life."

Roberta was indeed reaching people in this quaint upper room. Here many famous people came to "sit at her shrine." She reached the famous and the ordinary with her rock, soul, folk and jazz. One Sunday afternoon the entire Washington Commission on the Arts dropped in to hear her.

The drop-in who probably made the most difference in Roberta's life was jazz-pianist Les McCann. One afternoon in 1968 Roberta was doing a benefit for a ghetto children's library. McCann was playing at the Bohemian Caverns and came to check her out on his night off.

From that moment on, Roberta became a public figure —

Roberta Flack — talented and trained musician,
Roberta Flack — warm and enchanting performer,
Roberta Flack — star with millions of records sold,
Roberta Flack — black artist with an expressed
commitment to human rights.

"As strongly as I believe in the black struggle," Roberta once told an interviewer, "or anyone's struggle for equality and just basic human rights, I know that my best bet is to express this through music." At another time she said, "You see, that's the thing today. This communication — oneness — has to come out in music."

JACKSON FIVE
CARLY SIMON
BOB DYLAN
JOHN DENVER
THE BEATLES
ELVIS PRESLEY
JOHNNY CASH
CHARLEY PRIDE
ARETHA FRANKLIN
ROBERTA FLACK
STEVIE WONDER

# Rock'n PopStars